SECOND EDITION
Workbook **1**

Herbert Puchta · Peter Lewis-Jones · Günter Gerngross · Helen Kidd

CAMBRIDGE
UNIVERSITY PRESS

Contents

Friends   4

1 At School   10

2 Let's Play   22

3 Pet Show   34

4 Lunchtime   46

5 Free Time   58

6 The Old House   70

7 Get Dressed   82

8 The Robot   94

9 At the Beach   106

Picture Dictionary   118

Friends

1 **Read and match. Color the circles.**

1 ● I'm Whisper. 2 ○ I'm Flash. 3 ○ I'm Thunder. 4 ○ I'm Misty.

1 Look and match.

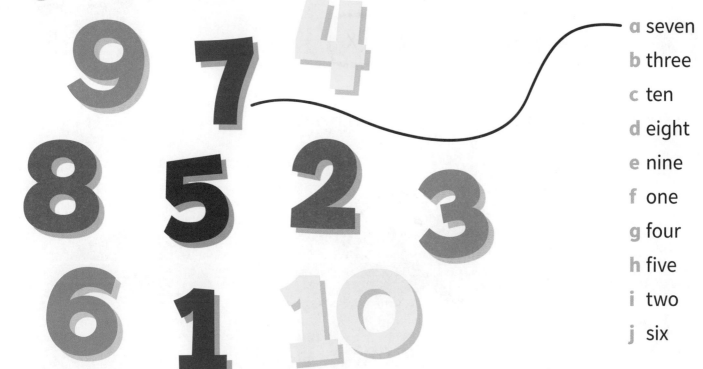

9   7   4

8   5   2   3

6   1   10

a seven
b three
c ten
d eight
e nine
f one
g four
h five
i two
j six

2 Write the number words.

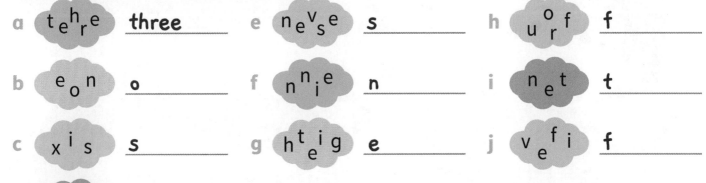

a three

b o _____

c s _____

d t _____

e s _____

f n _____

g e _____

h f _____

i t _____

j f _____

3 Look. Then write about you.

1 What's your name?

I'm _____.

2 How old are you?

I'm _____.

I'm Sam.
I'm six.

1 🎧 01 Can you remember? Listen and write.

E   G   T   Q   X

1 Color the words.

purple orange
yellow red
green blue

2 Write your name. Then draw a picture of you.

Hi, I'm _____.

1 🎧 02 **Who says it? Listen and check the box ☑.**

1  ☐ ☐

2  ☐ ☐

3  ☐ ☐

2 **Match the Super Friends with the powers.**

1

2

3

4

a

b

c

d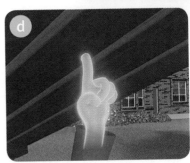

1 Write and circle.

1 I can write the names of ten numbers.   Yes / No

one _____   _____   _____   _____   _____

_____   _____   _____   _____   _____

2 What color is the balloon?

The balloon is green / red.

3 What color is the bag?

The bag is blue / purple.

2 Write the letters.

In the alphabet …

1 what's after "B"? C

2 what's after "E"? ____

3 what's before "K"? ____

4 what's after "M"? ____

5 what's before "R"? ____

6 what's before "T"? ____

  3 Read. Then draw and write.

Hi! I'm Alex. I'm six.

My bag is yellow. Look!

_____

_____

1 At School

1 Look and match.

1 desk
2 bag
3 pencil
4 notebook
5 eraser
6 book
7 pen
8 paper
9 ruler
10 pencil case

2 Look and color.

1
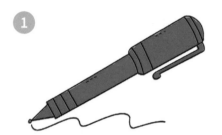

2
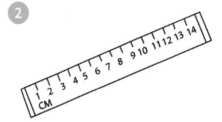

3
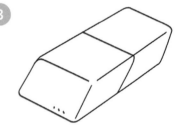

4
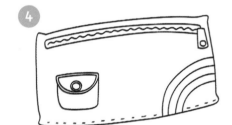

5

6

Key

1 **Look and write.**   is   isn't   it   ~~this~~

① What's **this** _____?

② Is _____ a pencil?

③ No, it _____.

Is it a ruler?

④ Yes, it _____.

2 **Read and check the box ☑.**

1 What's this? Is it a desk?

☐ Yes, it is.   ☑ No, it isn't.

2 What's this? Is it a pencil case?

☐ Yes, it is.   ☐ No, it isn't.

3 What's this? Is it a pencil?

☐ Yes, it is.   ☐ No, it isn't.

4 What's this? Is it an eraser?

☐ Yes, it is.   ☐ No, it isn't.

1   **Can you remember? Listen and write.**

What's this? What's this? Please tell me, what's this?

(1) Is it a  pen_____? (2) Is it a _____?

Come on, take a look.

(3) It's a _____ ... (4) It's a _____ ...

2 **Look and write.**

1 Is it a bag?

No, it isn't._____

2 Is it a book?

Yes,_____

3 Is it a pen?

_____

 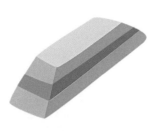 

4 Is it a ruler?

_____

5 Is it an eraser?

_____

6 Is it a pencil case?

_____

1 **Write the words.** | get | Open | ~~Sit~~ | Write

(1) __Sit_____ at your desk, please.

(2) Now _____ a pen.

(3) _____ your book, please.

(4) _____ one to ten.

2 **Look and number the pictures.**

1. Open your book, please.
2. Write one to ten.
3. Now get a pen.
4. Sit at your desk, please.
5. Close your bag, please.
6. Pass me a pen, please.

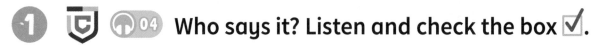

1 🛡 🎧 04 **Who says it? Listen and check the box ☑.**

2 🛡 **Look and check ☑ or put an X in the box ☒.**

In the story, Flash's friends have …

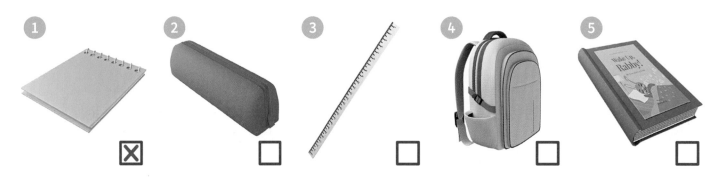

1 ☒ 2 ☐ 3 ☐ 4 ☐ 5 ☐

3 🛡 **Who says it? Match.**

1 Flash, come back!

2 Pass me the box, please.

3 Here's your book.

4 Watch out!

a   b   c   d

1 **Who says what? Write numbers.**

1 Here's your book.

2 Watch out!

3 I'm sorry.

2 🎧 05 **Write and match. Listen and say.**

1 A c **a t**

2 A f_ _t r_ _t

3 A bl_ _ck h_ _t

4 A bl_ _ck b_ _g

 1

1 Look and read. Check ☑ or put an X in the box ☒.

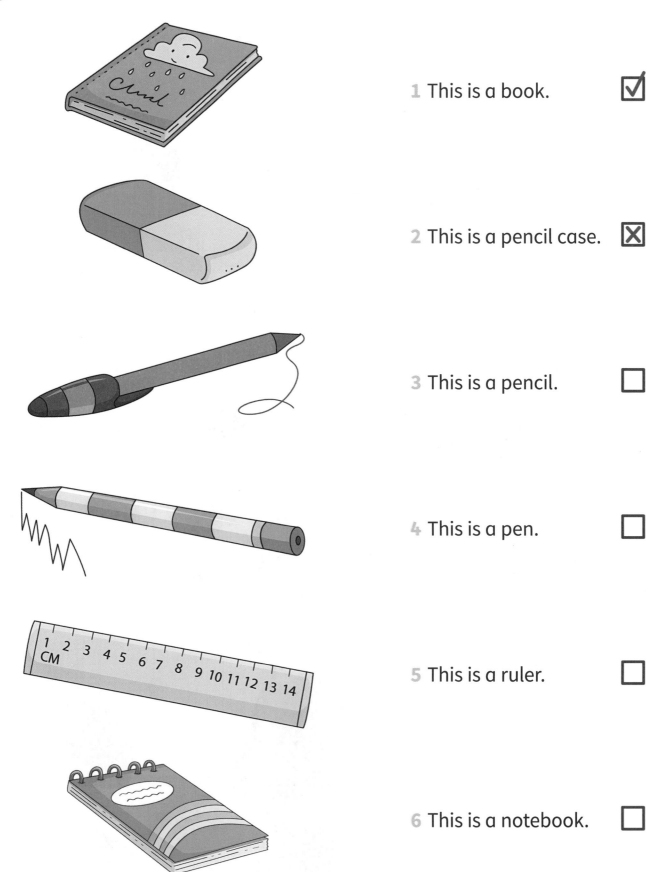

1 This is a book. ☑

2 This is a pencil case. ☒

3 This is a pencil. ☐

4 This is a pen. ☐

5 This is a ruler. ☐

6 This is a notebook. ☐

1 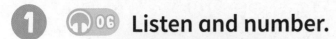 **Listen and number.**

2 **Draw and write about your pencil case.**

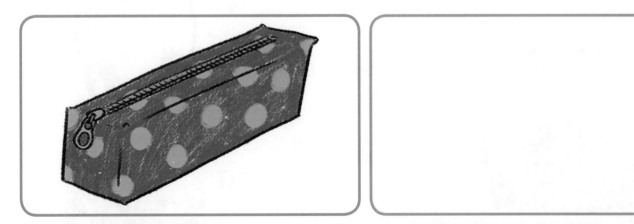

This is my pencil case.

It's blue and pink.

_____

Senses

1 **Look and write.**

| look | listen | ~~smell~~ | taste | touch |

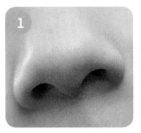   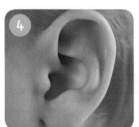 

smell _____ _____ _____ _____

2 **Look and match.**

1

a taste

b look

2

3

c smell

d touch

4

5

e listen

3 **Look and write.**

| Look | Listen | Taste |

1

_____ to this song!

2

_____ at this shell!

3

_____ this ice cream!

4 **Choose and draw.**

| look | listen | ~~smell~~ | taste | touch |

_____smell_____

_____

1 **Make a pencil holder.**

You need

toilet
paper tube

scissors

cardboard

glue

magazines

1
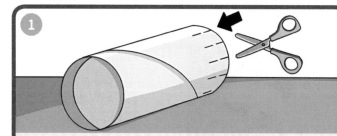
Cut flaps at the bottom of the
toilet paper tube.

2
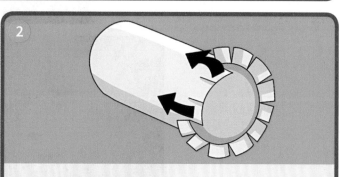
Fold the flaps out.

3
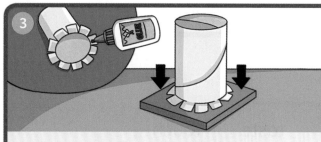
Glue the flaps on the piece of
cardboard.

4

Cut out pictures from magazines.

5

Glue the pictures on the tube.

6

Now you have a pencil holder.

1 **Write and circle.**

1 I can write the names of five classroom objects.   Yes / No

pen _____   _____   _____   _____   _____

2 What's this? Is it an eraser ?

Yes, it _____ . / No, it _____ .

3 What's this? Is it a notebook?

Yes, it _____ . / No, it _____ .

2 **Look and write.**

BIG QUESTION How do we learn?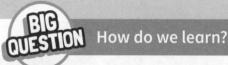

 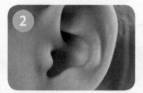 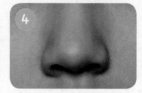 

l _ook_ _____   l _____   t _____   s _____   t _____

3   **Read. Then draw and write.**

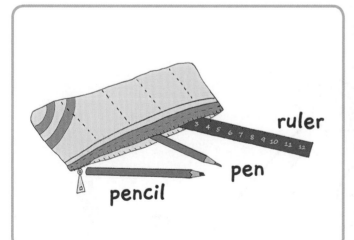

ruler

pen

pencil

This is my pencil case.

It's yellow and green.

_____

_____

2 Let's Play

1 Look and number.

1 train   2 plane   3 monster   4 kite   5 bike

6 ball   7 doll   8 car   9 computer game   10 go-kart

2 Connect the dots. What is it? Write.

It's a _____.

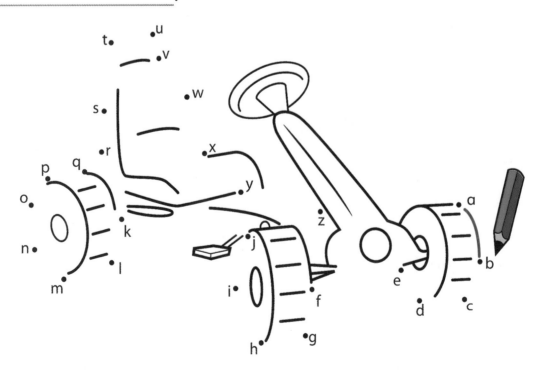

1 Draw lines and write.

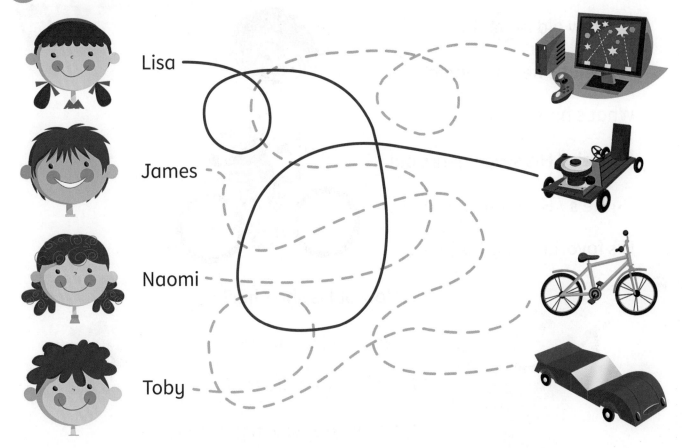

1 Her name's Lisa. Her favorite toy is her __go-kart__ .

2 His name's James. His favorite toy is his _____ .

3 Her name's Naomi. Her favorite toy is her _____ .

4 His name's Toby. His favorite toy is his _____ .

2 Read and match.

1 What's his name?

2 How old is he?

3 What's his favorite toy?

4 What's her name?

5 How old is she?

6 What's her favorite toy?

a He's ten.

b She's eight.

c His name is Ben.

d Her name is Kate.

e Her favorite toy is her plane.

f His favorite toy is his train.

1 Can you remember? Listen and circle.

(1) How old is **he** / **his**?

(2) What's **he** / **his** name?

What's his favorite toy?

(3) **He's** / **His** seven years old.

(4) **He's** / **His** name is Mike.

His favorite toy is his bike …

(5) How old is **she** / **her**?

(6) What's **she** / **her** name?

What's her favorite toy?

(7) **She's** / **Her** seven years old.

(8) **She's** / **Her** name is Jane.

Her favorite toy is her plane.

2 Draw and write about you.

My name is

_____.

I'm _____
years old.

My favorite toy is
my _____.

1 **Look, read, and check the box ☑.**

1 an old car
    a  ☐   b  ☑

2 an ugly monster
    a  ☐   b  ☐

3 a short plane
    a 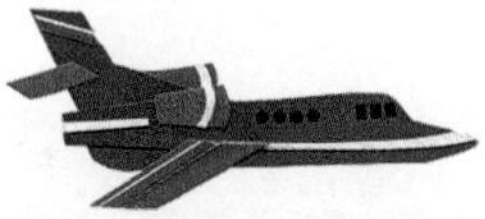 ☐   b 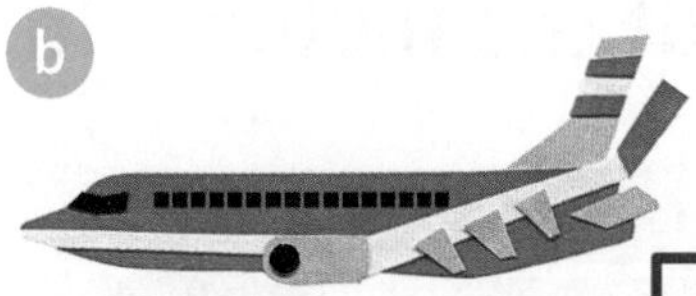 ☐

4 a small kite
    a  ☐   b ☐

2 **Write the words in the correct order.**

big   a   white   ball

1 a big white ball

train   blue   a   long

2 _____

bike   a   new   red

3 _____

1 🎧 08 Who says it? Listen and check the box ☑.

2 🛡 Put the pictures in order. Write numbers.

1   **Who says it? Check the box of ☑ the correct picture.**

That isn't fair!

2 🎧 09 **Write *e* or *a*. Listen and say.**

1 c **a** t   **2** p___n   **3** p___ncil   **4** b___g

5 d___sk   **6** t___n   **7** bl___ck   **8** Fl___sh

1 🎧 **10** **Listen and color.**

2 🛡 **Look and write.**

<u>Her favorite things</u>

Her favorite **number is four**_____.
Her favorite _____
_____.
Her favorite _____
_____.

1 Read, number, and color.

1 a big yellow doll

2 a long blue train

3 an ugly green monster

4 a new black bike

5 a short red train

6 an old purple bike

7 a beautiful black monster

8 a small pink doll

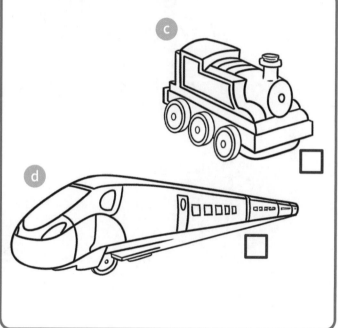

1 **Look and write.**

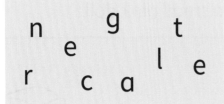

1 r e c t a n g l e   2 _ _ _ _ _ _ _ _ _ _

3 _ _ _ _ _ _ _   4 _ _ _ _ _ _ _ _   5 _ _ _ _

2 **Look and match.**

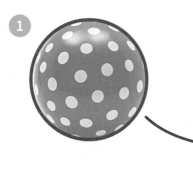
1

a triangle

b kite

c rectangle

d circle

e square

2

3

4

5

3 Which shapes are in the toys? Look and check ✓ or put an X in the box ☒.

1

a triangle ✓
b kite ☒
c circle ✓

2

a square ☐
b triangle ☐
c kite ☐

3

a rectangle ☐
b square ☐
c circle ☐

4 Read and look at Activity 3. Write the names of the toys.

1 A triangle and two circles.   bike

2 A square, a rectangle, and two circles. _____

3 A kite and four triangles.   _____

5 Choose, write, and draw.

> rectangle   square   circle   ~~triangle~~   kite

triangle

1 Make a paper kite.

You need

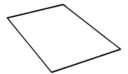 paper   markers   stapler   hole punch   string

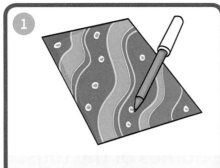

1. Color the paper.

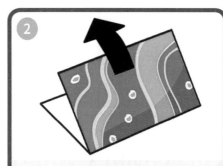

2. Fold the paper in half.

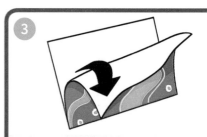

3. Bend one side of the paper.

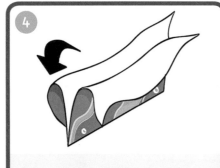

4. Bend the other side.

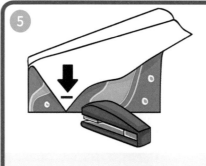

5. Staple the corners.

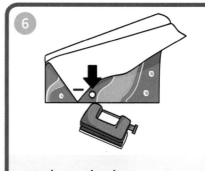

6. Make a hole.

7. Put the string through the hole and tie a knot.

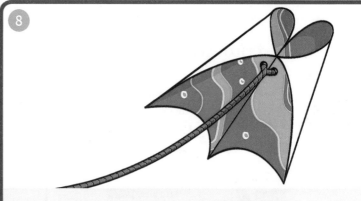

8. Now you have a paper kite.

1 **Write and circle.**

1 I can write the names of five toys.   Yes / No

__train__   _____   _____   _____   _____

2 What's his name?   He's / His name is Tom.

3 How old is he?   He's / His seven.

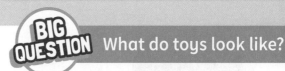
2 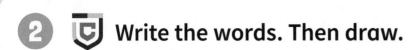 **Write the words. Then draw.**

BIG QUESTION   What do toys look like?

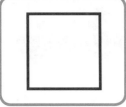    

1 s__quare__   **2** r__e____   **3** c__i____   **4** t r_____   **5** k__i____

 3 **Read. Then draw and write.**

rectangle

circle

My favorite toy is my car.   _____

It's an old red car.   _____

3 Pet Show

1 **Look and write.**

cat   dog   donkey
duck   elephant   frog
~~spider~~   lizard   rat

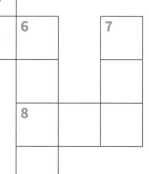

	1 s		2		
	p				
	i				
	3 d				
	e				
4	5		6	r	7
			8		

9

2 **Write and draw.**

My favorite animal is a _____. Look!

1 **Look and check the box** ☑.

1 The elephant is under the car.	☑	Yes	☐	No
2 The cat is on the car.	☐	Yes	☐	No
3 The frog is in the car.	☐	Yes	☐	No
4 The spider is on the car.	☐	Yes	☐	No
5 The duck is under the car.	☐	Yes	☐	No

2 **Look and write.**   on   in   under

(1) The frog's _____ my bag. **(2)** It's _____ my chair.

(3) It's not _____ my hat. It isn't there.

1   **Can you remember? Listen and write.**

(1) The frog's __on_____ a bag,

And that's not good.

(2) Put the _____ in the pond,

(3) Yes, the pond _____ the woods …

(4) The duck's _____ the car,

And that's not good.

(5) Put the _____ on the pond,

(6) Yes, the pond _____ the woods …

2 **Read, draw, and color.**

1 a rat in the pond   3 a dog in the bag   5 a cat on the bike

2 a duck on the pond   4 a lizard under the bike

1 Read and write the numbers.

a I like ducks. `4`

b I don't like frogs. ☐

c I like frogs. ☐

d I like lizards. ☐

e I don't like lizards. ☐

f I don't like ducks. ☐

2 Write the words.

I like   I don't like

I like frogs. What about you?

1 _____ frogs, too.

2 _____ big frogs.

1 🎧 **12** **Who says it? Listen and check the box ☑.**

 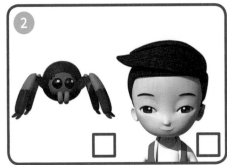 

2 🛡 **Look and match. Draw lines.**

1 He's amazing!

2 Touch him, Misty.

3 Look, he's under the table.

3 🛡 **Put the pictures in order. Write numbers.**

1 **Which boy is brave? Check ☑ the box for the correct picture.**

2 🎧 13 **Read, draw, and color. Listen and say.**

1 a **b**i**g** pa**n**

2 si**x** pe**n**s

3 a **p**i**nk** **d**esk

4 a **b**la**ck** r**at**

5 a re**d** **c**at

6 te**n** **b**a**g**s

1 Read and write the numbers.

a The elephant is under the tree. The lizard is on the elephant. ⬜ 4

b The elephant is in the pond. The spider is on the elephant. ⬜

c The elephant is under the tree. The spider is on the elephant. ⬜

d The elephant is in the pond. The lizard is on the tree. ⬜

2 Look and find three differences. Circle and write.

Picture 1	Picture 2
ten ducks	nine ducks

1 🎧 14 **Listen and draw lines.**

2 🛡 **Look at the picture in Activity 1 and write.**

1 The donkey is **under the tree** _____.

2 The duck is _____.

3 The dog is _____.

4 The cat is _____.

5 The spider is _____.

Think and Learn

Nature

1 **Look and write.**

air   food   ~~shelter~~   water

It needs …

shelter _____ _____ _____

2 **What does it need? Check ☑ the boxes.**

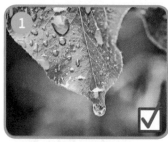 ☑

  ☐

 ☐

 ☐

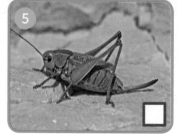  ☐

☐

3 🛡 **What is it? Write the numbers.**

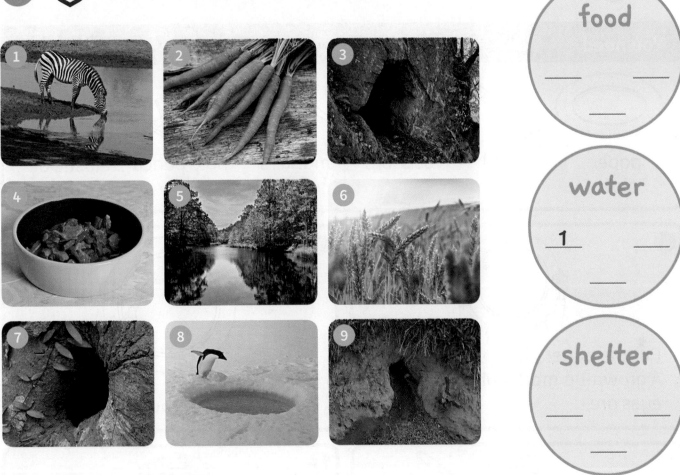

food
___ ___
___

water
_1_ ___
___

shelter
___ ___
___

4 🛡 **Draw and write about an animal.**

___Cat___

_____

It eats cat food. _____

It drinks water. _____

1 Make an animal mask.

You need

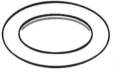 paper plate

 pencil

 scissors

 markers

 hole punch

 elastic or string

1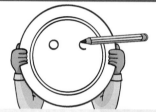
Put the paper plate on your face. A grown-up marks where your eyes are.

2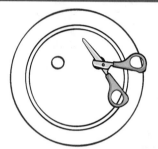
A grown-up cuts out the eyes.

3
Color the mask and draw a nose and a mouth.

4
A grown-up makes holes on the sides.

5
Tie elastic or string to the two sides.

6
Now you have an animal mask.

What do I know?

1 Write and circle.

1 I can write the names of five animals.   Yes / No

frog _____ _____ _____ _____

2 The dog is in / on the bag.

3 The cat is on / under the desk.

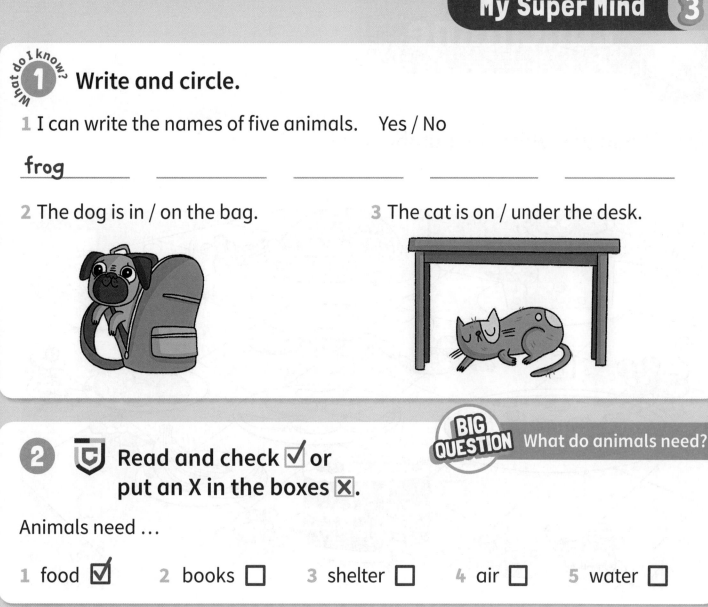

2 🛡 **Read and check ☑ or put an X in the boxes ☒.**

BIG QUESTION What do animals need?

Animals need …

1 food ☑   2 books ☐   3 shelter ☐   4 air ☐   5 water ☐

About me!

3 🛡 **Read. Then draw and write.**

I like lizards. _____

I don't like dogs. _____

1 Look and write the numbers.

1 pizza   2 chicken   3 apples   4 cheese

5 cake   6 sausages   7 bananas   8 carrots

2 🛡 Circle the food words.

steakcarrotfishrainbananascatpizzaapplebagpeas

1 Look and circle.

1 I (have) / don't have a sandwich.

2 I have / don't have a sausage.

3 I have / don't have an apple.

4 I have / don't have pizza.

5 I have / don't have a cake.

6 I have / don't have a banana.

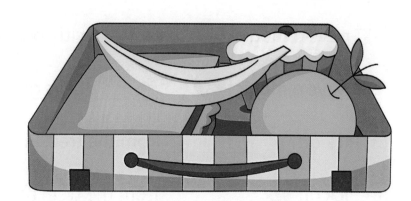

2 Read and match.

1 I have a banana and an apple. I don't have a carrot.

2 I have a banana and a carrot. I don't have an apple.

3 I have two carrots. I don't have a banana, and I don't have an apple.

4 I have two apples. I don't have a carrot, and I don't have a banana.

3 Look and write.

have   don't have

(1) I _____ a carrot.

(2) I _____ a carrot.

Look what I can do …

(3) Now I _____ a carrot!

1 🛡️ 🎧 **15** **Can you remember? Listen and write.**

(1) I have a magic 🌳 <u>**tree**</u> with lots of things to eat.

(2) I have a magic 🌳 _____ . Let's go and get a treat.

(3) Pick an 🍦 _____ from the tree. Pick an 🍑 _____ from the tree.

(4) Pick an 🍎 _____ from the tree. It's there for you and me.

(5) I have a magic 🌳 _____ with lots of things to take. 🎵

(6) I have a magic 🌳 _____ . Let's go and get a 🍰 _____ …

2 🛡️ **Which foods grow on trees? Draw.**

1 Who says what? Look and circle.

1 Penny, I'm hungry. Do we have any fish?

Paul / Penny

2 No, we don't. We don't have any fish.

Paul / Penny

3 Yes, we do! Yes, we have a fish.

Paul / Penny

2 Look at the picture and answer the questions.

1 Do we have any pizzas?

Yes, we do.

2 Do we have any peas?

No, we don't.

3 Do we have any steaks?

_____

4 Do we have any orange juice?

_____

3 Look and write questions.

1 **Do we have any apples?** _____

2 _____

3 _____

1 🎧 **16** **Who says it? Listen and check the box ☑.**

2 🛡 **Look and match. Draw lines.**

We have pizza.

①  ②

Pizza, please.

3 **Look and write.** What do you have?   Here you are.

Thank you.

I have a cheese sandwich.

1 **Read and match. Check the box for ☑ the correct picture.**

What is he doing? It's unfair!

2 🎧 17 **Listen and color. Point and say.**

Key   a = black   e = red   o = orange   i = pink

  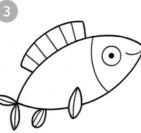 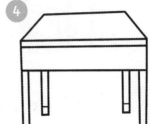

1 Look at the numbers. Look at the letters. Write the words.

1 **13** t h i r t e e n

2 **17** s _ _ _ _ _ _ _ _

3 **15** f _ _ _ _ _ _

4 **12** t _ _ _ _ _

5 **20** t _ _ _ _ _

6 **18** e _ _ _ _ _ _ _

2 Look and write.

1 twelve
   bananas

2 _____

3 _____

4 _____

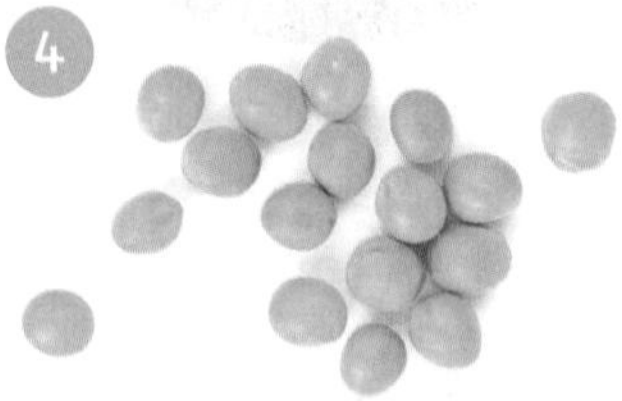

1 🎧 18 **Listen and check the box ☑.**

1 What's in the cake?

a  ☐

b  ☐

c  ☐

2 Where's the food?

a  ☐

b  ☐

c  ☐

2 🛡 **Read and match. Write numbers.**

1 I like pizza and peas. I don't like apples or milk.

2 I like pizza and carrots. I don't like bananas or milk.

3 I like sausages and carrots. I don't like bananas or orange juice.

4 I like sausages and peas. I don't like apples or milk.

a  ☐

b  ☐

c  ☐

d  1

Think and Learn

Food

1 **Look and write.**

> fruit   vegetables   plant   tree   ~~soil~~

soil _____   _____   _____   _____   _____

2 **Where does the food grow? Look and match. Then write** *fruit* **or** *vegetable* **under the pictures.**

vegetable _____   _____   _____

in the soil   on a plant   on a tree

_____   _____   _____

3 Put the pictures in order. Write numbers.

Now the carrot is **big** _____.

I eat the carrot. It's my _____!

The carrot is _____.

The carrot is _____.

4 Look at Activity 3. Write the words to complete the sentences.

> in a store   ~~big~~   in the soil   dinner

5 Find out about the food in your house. Draw and write.

> in the soil   on a plant   on a tree   fruit   vegetable

Food	🍎			
Fruit or vegetable?	fruit			
Where does it grow?	on a tree			

1 Make a place mat.

You need

 thin cardboard

 magazines

 scissors

 glue

 markers

1

Cut out pictures of food from magazines.

2

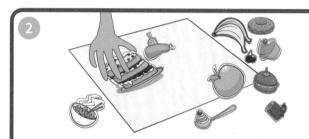

Think about where to put the pictures on the cardboard.

3

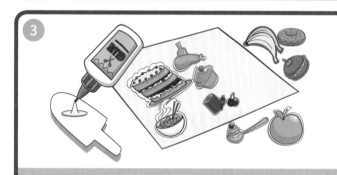

Glue the pictures on the cardboard.

4

Draw a border.

5

Write your name.

6

Now you have a place mat.

Write and circle.

1 I can write the names of five foods. Yes / No

sausage _____ _____

_____ _____

2 Do they have any pizzas?

Yes, they _____. / No, they _____.

2 **Look, read, and circle.**

 BIG QUESTION Where does food come from?

It grows …

1

in the soil / on a tree

2

on a tree / in the soil

3

in the soil / on a plant

 3 **Read. Then draw and write.**

My Lunch

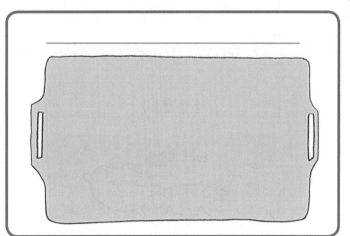

I have a cheese sandwich
and a banana.

5 Free Time

1 Write the days of the week.

1. aFiyrd
F r i d a y

2. ndSayu
_ _ _ _ _ _

3. dnesWayed
_ _ _ _ _ _ _ _ _

4. Sdyaatur
_ _ _ _ _ _ _ _

5. ayueTsd
_ _ _ _ _ _ _

6. shTdyaur
_ _ _ _ _ _ _ _

7. yMoadn
_ _ _ _ _ _

2 Draw your favorite day and write.

Friday

My favorite day is Friday. _____

1 Look, read, and match. Write numbers.

On Saturdays, …

a [2] b [ ] c [ ] d [ ]

1 I play with my toys.   3 I ride my horse.

2 I play computer games.   4 I go swimming.

2 Write the words in the correct order.

1 I / Sundays / ride / on / horse / my   I ride my horse on Sundays .

2 Fridays / I / piano / play / on / the   _____ .

3 Saturdays / go / I / on / swimming   _____ .

4 play / Tuesdays / soccer / on / I   _____ .

5 on / I / my / Wednesdays / ride / bike   _____ .

3 Write the words.   [like   go   play]

(1) I _____ swimming
on Mondays, swimming in the ocean.

(2) I _____ soccer on Tuesdays.
Come and play with me! …

(3) But on Saturdays and Sundays,
I _____ being with you.

Can you remember? Listen and draw lines.

1 Monday

2 Tuesday

3 Wednesday

4 Friday

5 Saturday

6 Sunday

2 **What do you do? Write and draw a picture.**

On Mondays, I _____

_____.

On Tuesdays, I _____

_____.

On Sundays, I _____

_____.

1 Read and circle the correct words.

1 Do you watch TV on the weekend?   No, I **do** / **don't**.

2 Do you ride your bike with Paul?   Yes, I **do** / **don't**.

2 Read and match. Then write answers.

a

1 Do you play soccer on the weekend? <u>Yes, I do.</u>

b

2 Do you sing songs on the weekend? <u>No, I don't.</u>

c

3 Do you play computer games on the weekend? _____

d

4 Do you ride a horse on the weekend? _____

5 Do you play the piano on the weekend? _____

f

e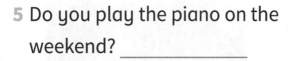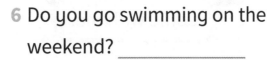

6 Do you go swimming on the weekend? _____

3 🛡 Write and check the box ✓.

	Yes, I do.	No, I don't.
1 Do you <u>ride</u> your bike on the weekend?	☐	☐
2 Do you _____ fishing on the weekend?	☐	☐
3 Do you _____ TV on the weekend?	☐	☐

1 🎧 **20** **Who says it? Listen and check the box ☑.**

2 🛡 **Look and write the numbers.**

1. Are you OK, Rabbit?

3. Watch out!

5. Rabbit, we're lost.

2. I don't know.

4. Here you are, Rabbit.

Yippee!

3

_____

Come with me.

_____

Where's the lake?

_____

_____

1   **Look and write.** | We're lost. Come with me.

_____

_____

2 **21 Write the words. Listen and say the sentences.**

rat   ~~lunch~~   milk   markers   eraser   dog

Mom and her **lunch** .

Ken and his _____ .

Jill and her _____ .

Polly and her _____ .

Sam and his _____ .

Gus and his _____ .

1 **Read and draw lines to make sentences.**

1 On Mondays, I play with
2 On Tuesdays, I ride
3 On Wednesdays, I play
4 On Thursdays, I go
5 On Fridays, I ride my
6 On Saturdays, I play the
7 On Sundays, I watch

a computer games.
b horse.
c piano.
d my friends.
e TV.
f swimming.
g my bike.

2 **Look at Activity 1. Write the days.**

a
b
c
d

Tuesday _____ _____ _____

e
f
g

_____ _____ _____

1 🎧 22 **What do they do? Listen and check the box ☑.**

1 On Mondays, James …

2 On Wednesdays, Emma …

3 On Fridays, Charles …

4 On Saturdays, Hannah …

2 🛡 **Look at Activity 1 and write the names.**

1 __James_____ plays soccer on Mondays.

2 _____ watches TV on Fridays.

3 _____ plays with her friends on Wednesdays.

4 _____ rides her horse on Saturdays.

Think and Learn

Activities

1 **Look and write.**

go climbing	go running	go skiing
go sledding	go surfing	~~go swimming~~

go swimming

2 **Where can we do it? Look and write the numbers.**

a
1

b

1 go climbing

2 go running

3 go skiing

4 go sledding

5 go surfing

6 go swimming

3 Read, look, and match.

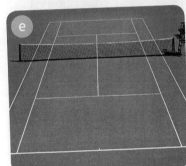

1 We ride a horse here.

2 We play soccer here.

3 We go fishing here.

4 We go running here.

5 We go climbing here.

6 We play tennis here.

4 What do they do? Look and write.

1 I *go swimming* .

2 I _____ .

3 I _____ .

4 I _____ .

1 **Make a guitar.**

You need

tissue box   paint and brushes   rubber bands of different sizes

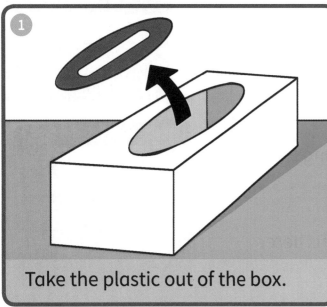

1 Take the plastic out of the box.

2 Paint the box.

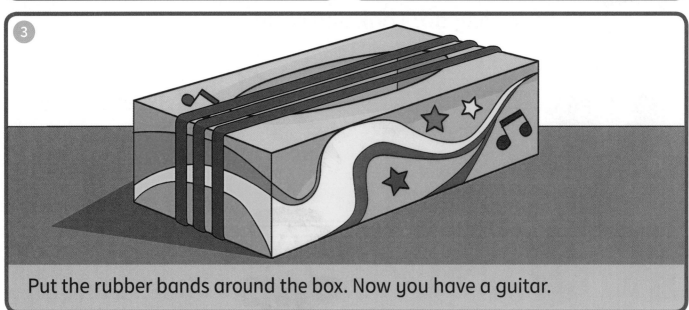

3 Put the rubber bands around the box. Now you have a guitar.

1 *What do I know?* **Write and circle.**

1 I can write the names of the days of the week.   Yes / No

Monday _____   _____   _____   _____

_____   _____   _____

2 Do you watch TV on the weekend?   Yes, I _____ . / No, I _____ .

2  **Look and read. Check ☑ or put an X in the box ☒.**   **BIG QUESTION** Which activities do we do?

 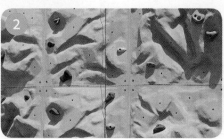 

We go skiing here. ☐   We go surfing here. ☐   We go running here. ☐

3 *About me!* **Read. Then draw and write.**

On Saturdays, I play soccer. _____   _____

_____

6 The Old House

1 Write the words.

bathroom   basement   stairs   kitchen
living room   ~~hall~~   bedroom   dining room

1
2
3
4

hall   _____   _____   _____

5
6
7
8

_____   _____   _____   _____

2 🛡 Choose a room. Write and draw.

Me in My Living Room

_____

1 Look and circle.

1

(**There's**) / **There are** a frog on the piano.

2

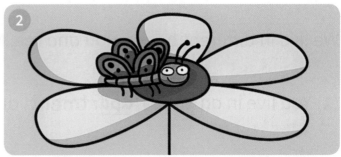

There's / **There are** a butterfly on the flower.

3

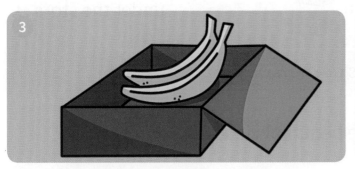

There's / **There are** bananas in the lunchbox.

4

There's / **There are** a lizard on the log.

5

There's / **There are** apples on the tree.

6

There's / **There are** a soccer ball on the TV.

2 Write the words.

There are   There's

(1) _____ a fish in the hall …

(2) _____ three fish in the kitchen.

1 🛡 🎧 **23** **Can you remember? Listen and write.**

We live in different house, you and me. Me and you. You and me …

(1) You live in an 🏢 <u>apartment</u>, and I live in a 🌳 _____!

(2) Some people live in houses. Some people live in 🚗 _____,

(3) Some people live in apartments, or in ⛺ _____ under the stars …

Some houses are very old. Some houses are new,

Some houses are very small. Some have beautiful views …

2 🛡 **Read and circle. Draw two houses.**

Some houses are **old** / **new**.

Some houses are **big** / **small**.

1 **Complete the questions.**

| Are | ~~Is~~ | How many | Is there | Are there |

(1) __Is_____ there a park?   No, there isn't.

(2) _____ a school?   Yes, there is.

(3) _____ there any trees?   No, there aren't.

(4) _____ any houses?   Yes, there are.

(5) _____ are there?   There are two.

2 **Look and write *Yes* or *No*. Then circle.**

1 Is there a butterfly on a flower?   __Yes____, there (is)/ **isn't**.

2 Are there any bananas on the tree?   _____, there **are** / **aren't**.

3 Is there a frog on the log?   _____, there **is** / **isn't**.

4 Are there any bikes on the grass?   _____, there **are** / **aren't**.

1 🎧 **24** **Who says it? Listen and check the box ☑.**

2 **Look and write.**

The stairs to the basement!

Big spiders!

1 How many are there?

e_____t

2 How many are there?

t_____e

3 **What does Misty say? Look and write the numbers.**

1 You can come in   **2** house   **3** me

Misty: There's the old ☐. Let's go in.

Misty: Let me go in. Wait for ☐ here.

Misty: There's no problem. ☐.

1   **Who takes care of a friend? Check ☑ the correct box.**

2 🎧 25 **Write the words. Listen and say.**

> hat   hall   ~~house~~   hot   happy   hairy

1 a small __house__

2 a _____ spider

3 a big _____

4 a _____ girl

5 a _____ pizza

6 a blue _____

1 Look and read. Write *yes* or *no*.

1 The house has a basement.   yes

2 There are two boys and two girls.   no

3 There's a chair in the bathroom.   _____

4 There are three dolls in the bedroom.   _____

5 The dog has a ball.   _____

6 There's a guitar in the kitchen.   _____

2 Look at Activity 1. Read and match.

1 They play soccer here.   a in the kitchen

2 They have dinner here.   b in the bedroom

3 They play the piano here.   c in the yard

4 There's a desk here.   d in the living room

1 🎧 **26** Listen and color.

2 **Look at the picture in Activity 1 and complete the sentences.**

1 There _'s one_ bike.

2 There _____ cats.

3 There _____ soccer ball.

4 There _____ trees.

Think and Learn

Houses

1 **Look and write.**

| cave house | houseboat | ~~tree house~~ | yurt |

tree house _____   _____   _____

2 **Read and write the numbers.**

My house is on the water.   My house is in a tree.   My house is round.

a yurt ☐   **b** houseboat 1   **c** tree house ☐

3 **Read, match, and circle.**

1 Which house is it?

2 How many rooms are there?

3 What does it have?

4 What doesn't it have?

a There are **three** / **five** rooms.

b It has a **kitchen** / **hallway**.

c It doesn't have a **basement** / **living room**.

d It's a (**tree house**)/ **house boat**.

4 **Read. Write a poem puzzle. Decorate.**

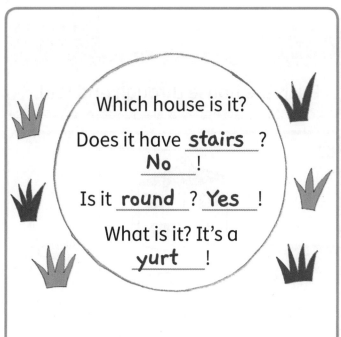

Which house is it?

Does it have **stairs** ?
No !

Is it **round** ? **Yes** !

What is it? It's a
yurt !

Which house is it?

Does it have _____ ?
_____!

Is it _____ ? _____!

What is it? It's a
_____!

1 **Make a pop-up house.**

You need

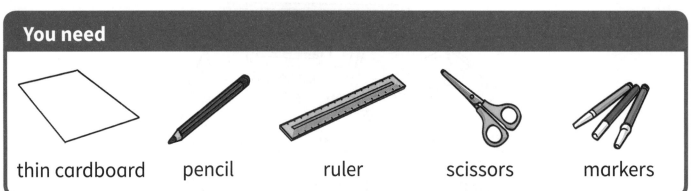

thin cardboard   pencil   ruler   scissors   markers

1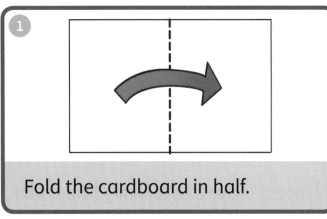

Fold the cardboard in half.

2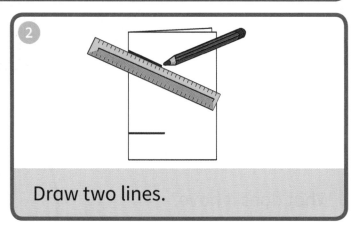

Draw two lines.

3

Cut along the lines.

4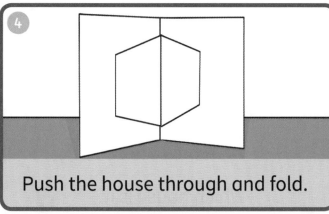

Push the house through and fold.

5

Open the cardboard. Color the house.

6

Now you have a pop-up house.

1 **Write and circle.**

1 I can write the names of five rooms in a house.   Yes / No

bedroom _____ _____ _____ _____

2 Are there any stairs in your house?

Yes, there _____. / No, there _____.

 2 **Write the words.**

BIG QUESTION How are houses different?

c _ave_   h _ouse_   h _____   y_____   t _____   h_____

3 **Read. Then draw and write.**

stairs   my bedroom   bedroom

bathroom   bedroom

My house has three
bedrooms and a bathroom.

_____
_____

7 Get Dressed

1 Find the clothes. Look → and ↓. Circle.

h	u	s	o	c	k	s	c	j	j	x
T	s	h	i	r	t	g	y	a	e	j
b	a	s	e	b	a	l	l	c	a	p
s	h	d	s	k	i	r	t	k	n	e
h	c	w	v	e	b	r	k	e	s	a
o	s	h	o	r	t	s	u	t	z	v
e	s	w	e	a	t	e	r	f	m	o
s	p	a	n	t	s	e	r	s	l	k

2 Look and write the words from Activity 1.

1.
2.
3.
4.
5.

socks _____

6.
7.
8.
9.
10.

_____

1 Read and write the numbers.

a I like these shorts.　　　③

b I like this T-shirt.　　　☐

c I don't like this T-shirt.　　☐

d I don't like these shorts.　　☐

2 Circle the words.

1 Do you like **this** / (**these**) jeans?

2 Do you like **this** / **these** baseball cap?

3 Do you like **this** / **these** skirt?

4 Do you like **this** / **these** socks?

5 Do you like this sweater?
No, I **do** / **don't**.

6 Do you like these pants?
Yes, I **do** / **don't**.

3 Write the words.

| do | ~~this~~ | don't | these |

(1) Do you like **this** _____ hat?

(2) Yes, I _____.

(3) Do you like _____ shoes?

(4) No, I _____.

Can you remember? Listen and write.

(1) Do you like this _purple_ _sweater_ ?

(2) Do you like this big, _____ _____?

Yes, I like your hat and sweater. You look good like that …

(3) Do you like these _____ _____?

(4) Do you like this _____?

Yes, I like your cap and pants. You look good like that …

2 Read, draw, and color.

- a purple baseball cap

- yellow socks

- green shoes

- an orange sweater

- blue pants

- a red jacket

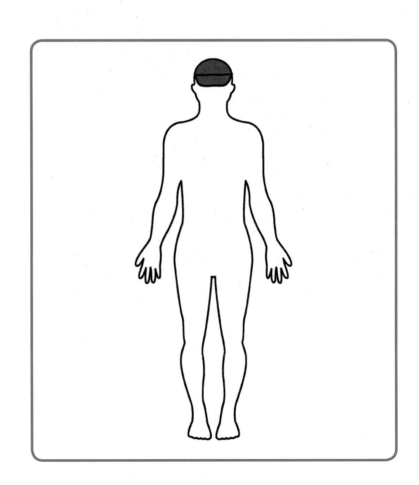

1 Read and look. Point to Sam.

Look, that's Sam!

Is he wearing a blue cap?

No, he isn't.

Is he wearing a red cap?

Yes, he is. Sam's wearing a red cap.

Wave to him!

Sam

2 Read and write the names under the pictures in Activity 1.

Kim is wearing a yellow sweater, blue shorts, and a yellow baseball cap.

Sam is wearing a white T-shirt, orange shorts, and a red baseball cap.

Tim is wearing a green jacket, blue jeans, and a blue baseball cap.

Jo is wearing a purple T-shirt and black jeans.

3 Look at the pictures in Activity 1. Read and circle *yes* or *no*.

1 Is Tim wearing jeans?   (yes)/ no

2 Is Jo wearing a baseball cap?   yes / no

3 Are Kim and Sam wearing shorts?   yes / no

4 Are Sam and Jo wearing jackets?   yes / no

Is he / she +ing? 85

1 🎧 28 **Who says it? Listen and check the box ☑.**

2 🛡 **Write the names. Who's wearing … ?**

1 these shoes?   **2** this cap?   **3** this skirt?

 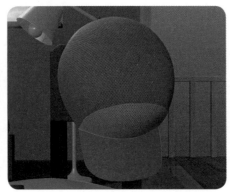 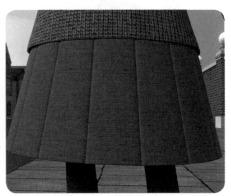

3 🛡 **Who says it? Match.**

1 Look! Gary's wearing my cap.

3 That's my cap!

2 No problem.

4 Maybe Gary has the same cap.

1   **Look and write.** | It's OK.　　I'm very sorry.

1 _____

2 _____

2 🎧 29 **Write the letters. Listen and say.**

sw　~~st~~　sk　st　sp　sch　st　sn

1 __**st**__ op

2 _____ ider

3 _____ eak

4 _____ eater

5 _____ irt

6 _____ airs

7 _____ ool

8 _____ ake

1 🎧 30 Listen and color.

2 Read and write the numbers.

a She's wearing a blue T-shirt and blue shorts. She's playing soccer. ☐

b He's wearing a white T-shirt. He's putting socks in a box. ☐

3 Write about pictures one and two in Activity 2.

1 He's **wearing a yellow baseball cap** . He's _____ .

2 She's _____ . She's _____ .

1 **Look at the pictures and read the questions. Write one-word answers.**

1 What's the boy doing?

He's _____.

2 Where are the boy and the girl?

In the _____.

3 What's the boy doing?

He's playing computer _____.

4 What's the girl doing?

She's watching _____.

5 How many cats are there?

There are _____.

6 Where are the cats?

Under the _____.

Patterns

1 **Look and write.**

| plain | stripes | ~~dots~~ | zigzags | flowers |

dots

2 **Read and match.**

1 a skirt with dots

2 a sweater with zigzags

3 plain jeans

4 shoes with flowers

5 socks with stripes

6 a plain jacket

3 🛡 **Design some pants. Then write.**

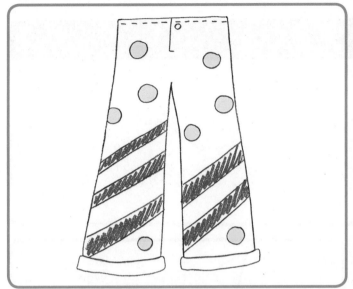

They're white pants with
red stripes and yellow dots.
_____

They're _____ pants
with _____ _____
and _____ _____.

4 🛡 **Find out about your clothes. Complete the chart.**

My Clothes

with dots	6 socks
with stripes	2 T-shirts
with zigzags	sweater
with flowers	shorts
plain	3 skirts

My Clothes

with dots	_____
with stripes	_____
with zigzags	_____
with flowers	_____
plain	_____

1 **Make a party hat.**

You need

| thin cardboard | stapler | colored paper | markers | scissors | glue |

1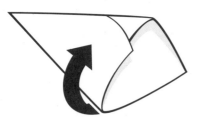
Make a hat shape with the cardboard.

2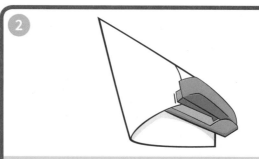
A grown-up staples the hat.

3
Cut out shapes and stick them on the hat.

4
Draw a pattern on the hat.

5
Now you have a party hat.

1 **Write and circle.**

1 I can write five names for clothes.   Yes / No

 pants   _____   _____

 _____   _____

2 Do you like this sweater with stripes?

 Yes, I _____ . / No, I _____ .

BIG QUESTION How do clothes look different?

2 **Draw patterns and write.**

1 s**tripes**   2 f_____   3 p_____   4 p_____   5 z_____

3 **Read. Then draw and write.**

I'm wearing a T-shirt with red
and white stripes, jeans,
and orange shoes.

_____
_____
_____
_____

8 The Robot

1 Make parts of the body. Write the letters. | s a d g e o |

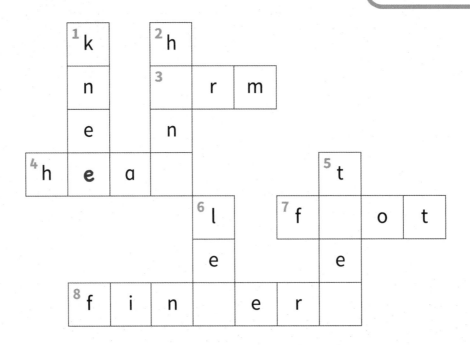

Crossword:
- 1 down: k n e
- 2 down: h n
- 3 across: h r m
- 4 across: h e a
- 5 down: t e
- 6 down: l e
- 7 across: f o t
- 8 across: f i n e r

2 Look and write.

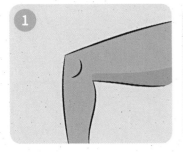  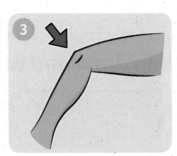 

leg _____   _____   _____   _____

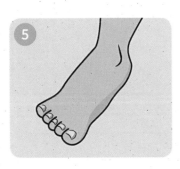 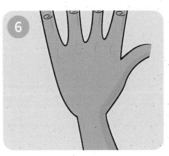 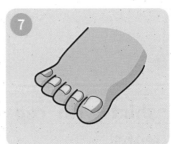 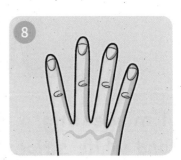

_____   _____   _____   _____

1 Read and write the numbers.

1 I can stand on one leg.

2 I can skip.

3 I can touch my toes.

4 I can't stand on one leg.

5 I can't skip.

6 I can't touch my toes.

2 What can Penny do? Write *can* or *can't*.

(1) I ___can___ stand on one leg …

(2) I _____ skip.

(3) I _____ swim.

(4) I _____ sing.

(5) But I _____ fly.

1 🛡 🎧 31 **Can you remember? Listen and write.**

(1) I can take my 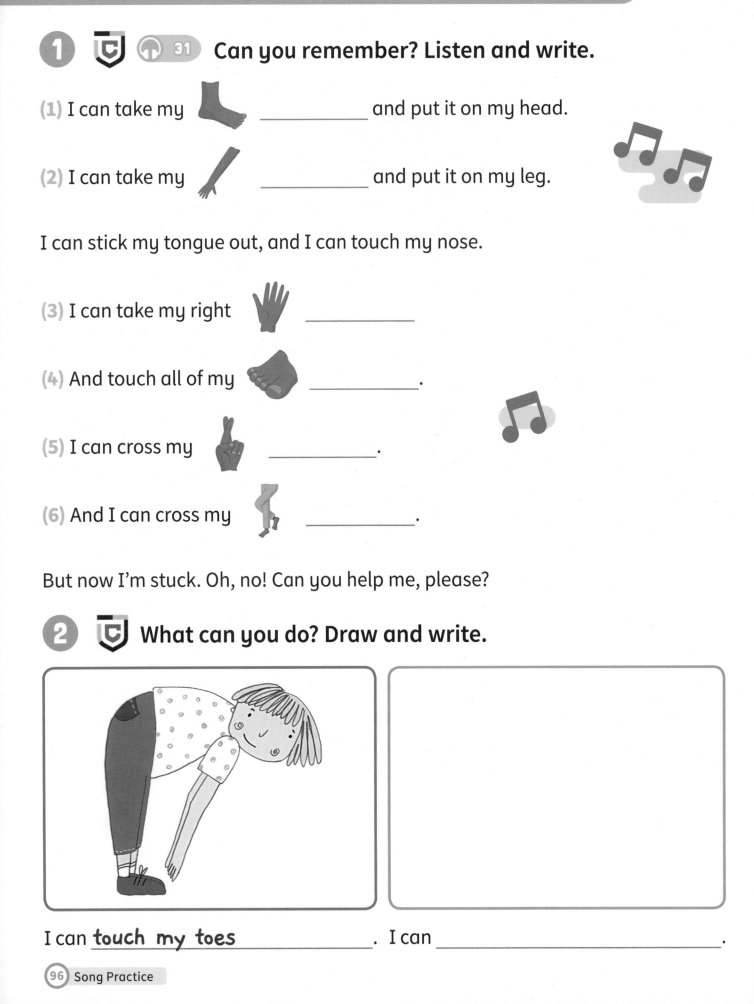 _____ and put it on my head.

(2) I can take my _____ and put it on my leg.

I can stick my tongue out, and I can touch my nose.

(3) I can take my right _____

(4) And touch all of my _____ .

(5) I can cross my _____ .

(6) And I can cross my _____ .

But now I'm stuck. Oh, no! Can you help me, please?

2 🛡 **What can you do? Draw and write.**

I can **touch my toes** _____ . I can _____ .

1 Look, write, and check ☑ the box.

1 <u>Can he</u> play the piano?

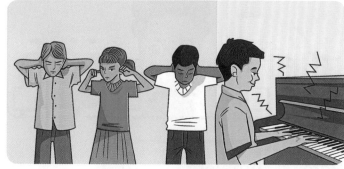

☐ Yes, he can.　☑ No, he can't.

2 _____ ride a bike?

☐ Yes, she can.　☐ No, she can't.

3 _____ swim?

☐ Yes, he can.　☐ No, he can't.

4 _____ ride a horse?

☐ Yes, she can.　☐ No, she can't.

2 Look and write the answer for you.

1 Can you cook?　**2** Can you draw?　**3** Can you dance?

<u>Yes</u>, I <u>can</u>.　_____, I _____.　_____, I _____.

1 🎧 32 Who says it? Listen and check ☑ the box.

1 □ □

2 □ □

3 □ □

2 Write the words.

done   Here   ~~problem~~   try

1

2 No **problem** .

3 _____ you are.

4

8 Good job _____ , Misty.

6 Let me _____ something.

7

3 🛡 Look at the pictures in Activity 2. Write the numbers.

a Thank you, Misty. 7

c We have a problem. □

b Batteries! We don't have batteries. □

d Thank you. □

1   **Which picture shows good teamwork? Check the box ☑.**

1

2

2 **Write and match. Listen and say.**

b

a

1 _**g**_ ray

2 fro____

3 computer ____ame

4 ____arden

5 fin____ers

6 le____

7 do____

d

c

g

e

f

1  Read and check ✓ or put an ☒.

Hi, I'm Ben. I can touch my toes, but I can't skip. I can play the piano, and I can play soccer But I can't play tennis. I can ride a bike, but I can't ride a horse.

Hi, I'm Anna. I can skip, but I can't touch my toes. I can play the piano, and I can play tennis But I can't play soccer. I can ride a bike, and I can ride a horse.

Hi, I'm Tom. I can touch my toes, and I can skip. I can play tennis, and I can play soccer But I can't play the piano. I can ride a bike, but I can't ride a horse.

	touch toes	skip	play the piano	play soccer	play tennis	ride a bike	ride a horse
Ben	✓						
Anna							
Tom							

2 Look at Activity 1. Write.

1 Ben, can you ride a bike? — Yes, I can.

2 Ben, can you skip? — No, I can't.

3 Anna, can you touch your toes? — _____

4 Anna, can you play tennis? — _____

5 Tom, can you ride a bike? — _____

6 Tom, can you play the piano? — _____

1 🎧 34 **Read the questions. Listen and write a name or a number.**

1 What's the girl's name?   Karen

2 How old is she?

3 What's the dog's name?

4 How many lizards does the girl have?

5 What's the horse's name?

Think and Learn

Movements

1 **Look and write.**

> forward   backward   stretch
> sideways   ~~step~~   jump

step _____

_____   _____   _____

2 **Read and draw lines. Write.**

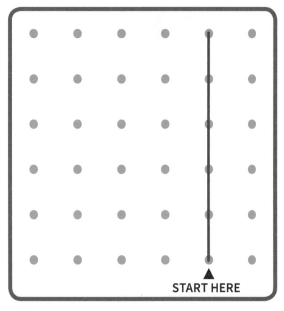

START HERE

1 Go five steps 👣 forward ↑ .

2 Go three steps 👣 sideways to the left ← .

3 Go five steps 👣 backward ↓ .

4 Go three steps 👣 sideways to the right → .

Look. What shape is it? It's a _____ .

3 🛡️ **Read and write the numbers.**

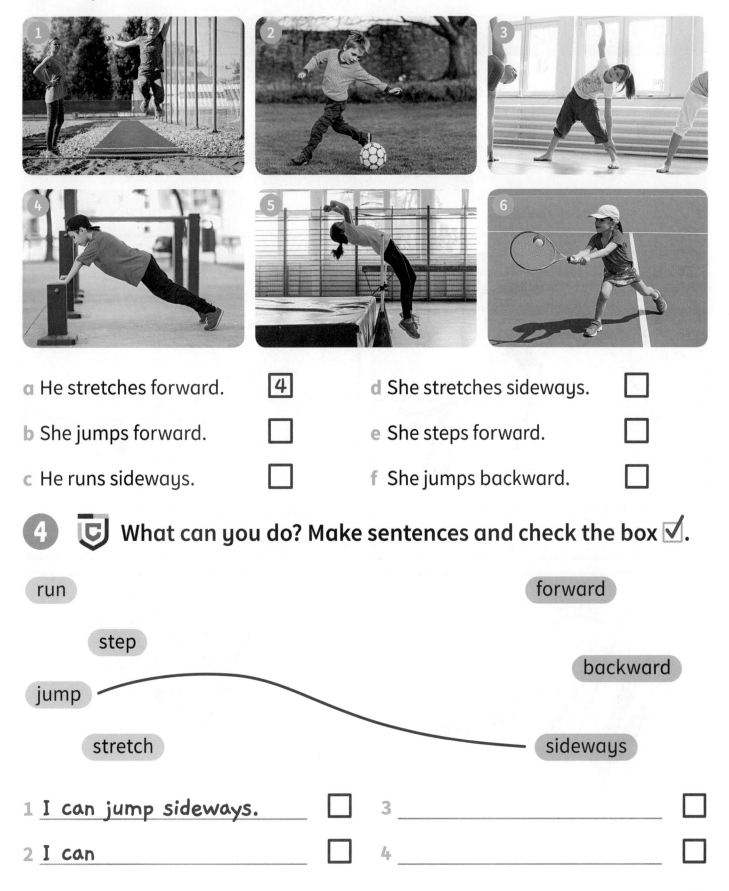

a He stretches forward. `4`

b She jumps forward. ☐

c He runs sideways. ☐

d She stretches sideways. ☐

e She steps forward. ☐

f She jumps backward. ☐

4 🛡️ **What can you do? Make sentences and check the box ☑.**

run   forward

step

                backward

jump

stretch   sideways

1 I can jump sideways. ☐   3 _____ ☐

2 I can _____ ☐   4 _____ ☐

1 🛡 **Make a robot mask.**

You need

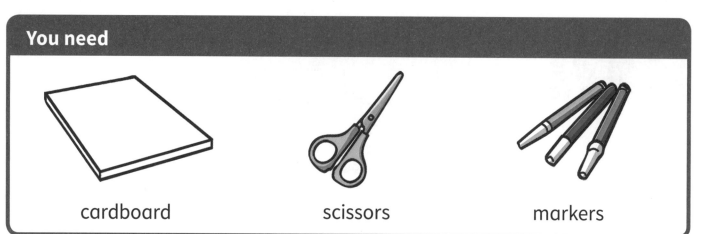

cardboard   scissors   markers

1

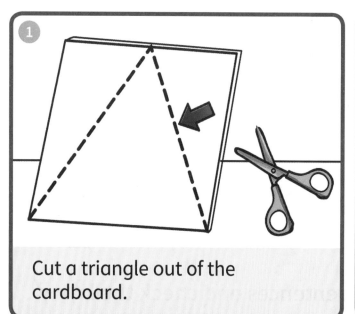

Cut a triangle out of the cardboard.

2

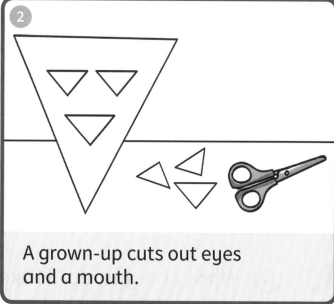

A grown-up cuts out eyes and a mouth.

3

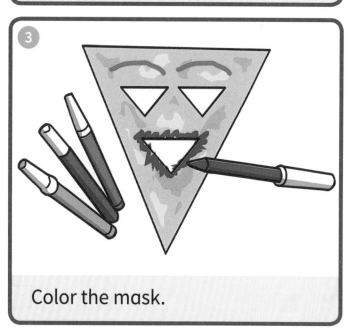

Color the mask.

4

Now you have a robot mask.

What do I know?

1 Write and circle.

1 I can write the names of five parts of the body.   Yes / No

__foot_____   _____   _____

_____   _____

2 Can you cross your legs?

Yes, I _____ . / No, I _____ .

2 Write the movement words.

BIG QUESTION How can we move?

1 r f o d / w a

f**orward**_____

2 k c w d r / a a b

b_____

3 e i s d w / a y s

s_____

4 p j u / m

j_____

5 s t / e p

s_____

3 Read. Then draw and write.

About me!

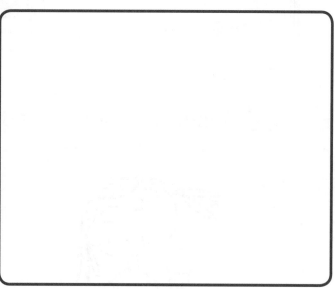

I can **run backward, but**_____   I can _____

I can't touch my toes_____ . _____ .

9 At the Beach

1 Write the words.

1
look for **shells**

2
take a _____

3
catch a _____

4
paint a _____

5
listen to _____

6
eat _____

7
read a _____

8
make a _____

9
play the _____

2 Read. Then write and draw.

I'm eating ice cream. _____

1 **Write the words.** make look read ~~listen~~ catch take

1 Let's _listen_ to music. Good idea.

2 Let's _____ a fish. I'm not sure.

3 Let's _____ some photos. Sorry, I don't want to.

4 Let's _____ a book. Good idea.

5 Let's _____ for shells. Sorry, I don't want to.

6 Let's _____ a sandcastle. Good idea.

2 **Look and match with Activity 1. Write the numbers.**

a [4]
b ☐
c ☐
d ☐
e ☐
f ☐

1 🛡 🎧 35 **Can you remember? Listen and write.**

(1) Let's go to the mountains and _climb a tree_ .

(2) Let's _____, you and me.

Vacation, vacation, vacation time is near.

Vacation, vacation, it's the end of the year!

(3) Let's go to the beach and _____.

(4) Let's _____, you and me.

Vacation, vacation …

(5) No! Let's stay at home and _____.

(6) Let's _____, just you and me.

Vacation, vacation …

2 🛡 **Write two more sentences for the song. Draw pictures.**

Let's _____
_____.

Let's _____
_____.

1 **Write the words.**

It's	They're	~~Where are~~	Where's

(1) __Where are__ my sunglasses? (2) _____ on my head!
(3) _____ my cap? (4) _____ on my head!

2 **Look and match.**

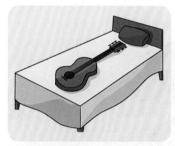   

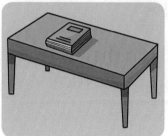   

1 Where's the guitar?

2 Where are the shells?

3 Where's the fish?

4 Where are the birds?

5 Where's the book?

6 Where's the shell?

7 Where's the picture?

8 Where's the ice cream?

a It's in the book.

b It's in the ocean.

c They're on the sandcastle.

d It's on his T-shirt.

e It's on the bed.

f It's on the sandcastle.

g It's on the desk.

h They're in the box.

1 🎧 36 **Who says it? Listen and check the box ☑.**

2 **Write the words.**

end   hill   ~~race~~   top

A **race** ?

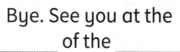

Bye. See you at the _____ of the _____!

This is the _____ of the race.

3 🛡 **Look and write the numbers.**

1 Let's go together.

2 What a good idea!

3 Let me try.

a _____

Thanks, Thunder.

Now you can race to the top, Flash!

b _____

No. ____. That's more fun!

c _____

Yes!

1   **Who shows modesty? Look and check the box for ☑ the correct picture.**

1
My picture's fantastic!

2
I really like your picture.

2 🎧 37 **Write *ee* or *ea* and match. Listen and say.**

a

b

1 s **ee** _____

2 r **ea** _____ d

3 thr_____

d

4 ch_____se

c

5 _____t

f

e

6 b_____ch

7 p_____s

h

g

8 ice cr_____m

1 **Read. Choose a word from the box. Write the correct word next to numbers 1–6.**

It's a beautiful day at the beach. The **(1)** <u>sun</u> is hot, and the **(2)** _____ is cool. There are lots of children. One boy is making a **(3)** _____ . It's very big. There's a little girl. She's wearing a **(4)** _____ on her head, and she's eating **(5)** _____ . There's a man. He's playing a **(6)** _____ .

What a beautiful day at the beach!

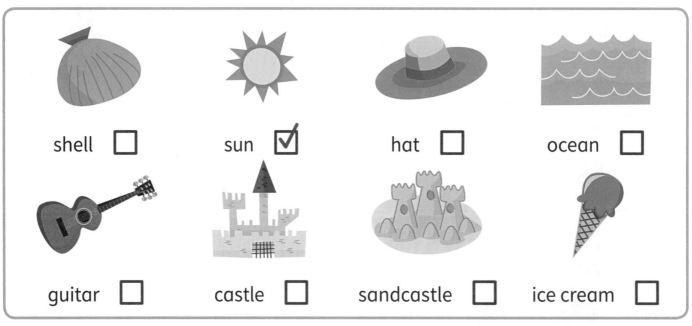

shell ☐   sun ☑   hat ☐   ocean ☐

guitar ☐   castle ☐   sandcastle ☐   ice cream ☐

1 🎧38 **Listen and number.**

1 Jim
2 Pip
3 Sue
4 Liz
5 Bob
6 Mia
7 Tom
8 Kay

2 🛡 **Look at the picture in Activity 1. Write the names.**

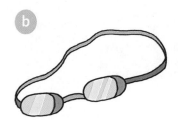

Liz _____

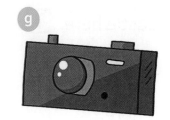
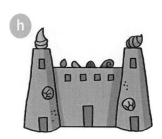

_____ _____ _____ _____

Think and Learn

Landscapes

1 **Look and write.**

| mountains | country | beach |
| ~~city~~ | theme park | campsite | lake |

city _____   _____   _____   _____

_____   _____   _____

2 **Read. Then look at the pictures in Activity 1. Write the numbers.**

a We can make a sandcastle here. 7

b We can climb up here. ☐

c We can sleep in a tent here. ☐

d We can go on a boat here. ☐

e We can ride on fun rides here. ☐

f We can see lots of trees here. ☐

g We can go to stores here. ☐

3 Read and match.

1 I'm in a city. I can take photos here.

2 I'm in the mountains. I can go skiing here.

3 I'm in the country. I can see birds here.

4 I'm at a campsite. I can sleep here.

5 I'm at the beach. I can go surfing here.

4 Choose, write, and draw.

the mountains   ~~the country~~
the beach   the city

I like **the country**.

I can **climb a tree** here.

I like _____.

I can _____ here.

1 Make a vacation scrapbook.

You need

 white paper

 colored paper

 hole punch

 string

 markers

 photographs

1
Put the white paper together.

2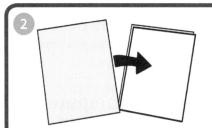
Put the colored paper on top.

3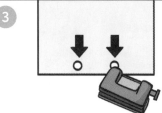
Make two holes in the paper.

4
Put the string through the holes. Tie a knot.

5
Draw a picture on the cover.

6
Draw pictures or stick in photographs. Write sentences.

7
Now you have a vacation scrapbook.

What do I know? 1 **Write and circle.**

1 I can write four things to do at the beach.   Yes / No

look for shells _____   _____

_____   _____

2 Let's listen to music. ☑   Good idea. / Sorry, I don't want to.

3 Let's play the guitar. ☒   Good idea. / Sorry, I don't want to.

---

2 **Draw places and write.**

BIG QUESTION Where can we go on vacation?

1 c ity _____   2 m _____   3 l _____

About me! 3 **Read. Then draw and write.**

My Vacation

I look for shells. _____

I eat ice cream. _____

Friends

nine   two   ~~one~~   seven   four
five   three   eight   ten   six

1   **2**   **3**

one _____

4   **5**   **6**   **7**

8   **9**   **10**

notebook ~~bag~~ ruler desk book
pencil case pencil eraser pen paper

bag _____ _____ _____

_____ _____ _____ _____

_____ _____ _____

2 Let's Play

car   doll   kite   ~~ball~~   computer game
plane   go-kart   bike   train   monster

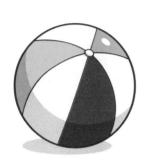

ball

3 Pet Show

rat   duck   frog   donkey   ~~cat~~
elephant   spider   dog   lizard

cat _____

_____

_____

_____

_____

_____

_____

_____

_____

4 Lunchtime

chicken   peas   carrots   pizza   cheese sandwich
~~apples~~   bananas   cake   steak   fish   sausages

  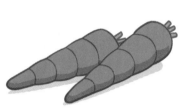 

apples

 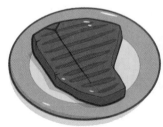 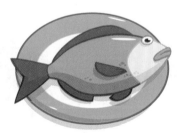 

nineteen ~~eleven~~ twelve eighteen fourteen
fifteen thirteen seventeen twenty sixteen

11 **12** **13**

eleven _____ _____

14 **15** **16** **17**

_____ _____ _____ _____

18 **19** **20**

_____ _____ _____

5 Free Time

Monday   Friday   Sunday   Tuesday
Wednesday   Saturday   Thursday

Monday

Tuesday

Wednesday

Thursday

Monday _____   _____   _____   _____

Friday

Saturday

Sunday

_____   _____   _____

6 The Old House

dining room   living room   basement   bedroom
kitchen   ~~bathroom~~   hall   stairs

bathroom

_____

_____

_____

_____

_____

_____

_____

7 Get Dressed

shorts   socks   jeans   ~~baseball cap~~   pants
skirt   T-shirt   shoes   jacket   sweater

baseball cap

_____

_____

_____

_____

_____

_____

_____

_____

_____

8 The Robot

leg   ~~arm~~   toes   head   fingers   hand   knee   foot

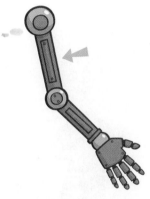

arm

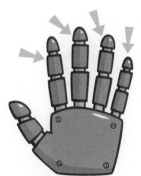

_____

_____

_____

_____

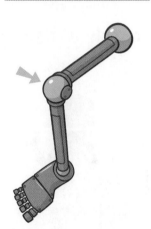

_____

_____

_____

paint a picture   ~~catch a fish~~   take a photo
listen to music   eat ice cream   play the guitar
read a book   look for shells   make a sandcastle

catch a fish

_____

_____

_____

_____

_____

_____

_____

_____